Cain a
and Sacrifice

*The Good News about Jesus,
from Genesis 4!*

Paul Taylor

J6D Publications

1

Published by:
J6D Publications
8141 Ackerman Drive
Pensacola, FL 32514
USA

ISBN: 978-1499520941

Contents

Foreword

By **Todd Friel**, host of Wretched Radio and Wretched TV (www.wretchedradio.com)

Movie critics so frequently use exaggeration that their words have no meaning:

Outlandishly funny, magnificently compelling, tremendously enlightening, profoundly inspiring. It is a shame that we have become desensitized to these words because the book you are holding deserves them all.

OK, it is not outlandishly funny, but it is definitely loaded with such powerful content that you will not put it down until you have drained every last drop. Even if you have read the Cain and Abel story a hundred times, you will find more gold in this book than the best movie ever made.

Introduction

The story of Cain and Abel was very familiar to me as a child. I was sent to Sunday school and I had lots of Bible story books around the house. *Cain and Abel* was therefore part of the staple diet of stories, with which I was familiar; along with *Adam and Eve*, *David and Goliath*, *Samson and Delilah*, *Daniel and the lions*, *Jonah and the whale* and many more. For all I knew, these could be no different from *Hansel and Gretel* or any other story.

Although I knew these stories, I had no idea about their connection, nor where they appeared in the history of God's people. No one had really told me about the Bible. I hadn't read it—although I had one—and therefore when I did eventually read the Bible in my late teens, I was amazed to find these stories in it! My Sunday School experience had not told me that there was a vast separation of time between many of these histories. So I did not understand the flow of God's work through all these stories.

Today, when I am talking to Sunday school teachers, I encourage them to use resources that teach not just the individual stories, but how they link together.

Cain and Abel, Worship and Sacrifice

"I have acquired a man from the LORD"

The story so far! God had created the world in six days and had rested on the seventh. He had made the world perfect. He had made a world in which there was no death or disease. He had made man in His own image, and had provided a wife for the first man, Adam, made from Adam's side. And He had given Adam and his wife, Eve, just one commandment—that they were not to eat of the fruit of the tree of knowledge of good and evil. On the day they broke that commandment, He warned them, the process of death would begin. Adam and Eve must have had sufficient language created in them, to understand this concept, even though they had not experienced it.

Yet Adam had broken God's command-ment. They had eaten the fruit they had been told not to eat. Eve had been tempted by the serpent, which was actu-ally the devil. This verse from Revela-tion—the last book of the Bible—shows the connection between the serpent and the devil.

> So the great dragon was cast out, that
> serpent of old, called the Devil and Satan,
> who deceives the whole world; he was
> cast to the earth, and his angels were
> cast out with him. (Revelation 12:9)

Following their sin, God pronounced three curses—one on the serpent, one on the woman and one on the man. When cursing the serpent, in Adam and Eve's hearing, God gave a remarkable and very important promise.

> And I will put enmity between you and
> the woman, and between your seed and
> her Seed; He shall bruise your head, and
> you shall bruise His heel. (Genesis 3:15)

The word translated as *bruise* is more to do with bruising ginger roots than bruising skin. It really refers to crushing. God is therefore promising that someone will come who will crush the serpent—though the serpent will crush his heel. This seems to be a reference to Jesus defeating Satan, by dying on the cross.

In every other part of the Old Testament, in the Hebrew language, "seed" always refers to a descendent of a man, not of a woman. Also, in biology we expect the seed to come from the man. So what does God mean by referring to the seed of the woman? Most commentators accept that Genesis 3:15 is the Bible's earliest statement of the Gospel, so it is likely that the seed of the woman means this: one day there was to come a man, who had an earthly mother, and was therefore human, but who had no earthly father, and therefore would not inherit the original sin from Adam. This man was to crush (bruise) the serpent's head, and therefore would have to be God Himself. This verse is therefore the first prophecy about the redemption of mankind through Jesus Christ.

Eve said "I have acquired a man from the LORD". Her words suggest that she believed what God was saying. Nevertheless, she misinterpreted God's words slightly. She had no concept of the idea that four thousand years would elapse before Jesus' birth. Why should she? She had never before experienced death, nor had she experienced childbirth. So it seems to me that when Cain was born, she actually thought that Cain could possibly be the Messiah.

So when Eve said "I have acquired a man from the LORD"—this being a pun on Cain's name, which means "acquired"—it would appear that, not only was Eve looking forward to the promised Saviour, the promised seed, but she actually thought that Cain might be that very seed! So Eve had high expectations for her first son. Cain did not live up to those expectations—he let her and his whole family down very badly, by becoming the world's first murderer.

"Abel was a keeper of sheep, but Cain was a tiller of the ground"

The second son of Adam and Eve mentioned in the Bible was Abel. The name Abel means *breath* or *nothing*. His name would seem to be a prophecy about the length of his life. His name is used elsewhere in the Bible as a word that means "meaningless". What was to be the point of Abel's life? He died young, killed by his brother, and his name meant nothing! Yet we shall see that his life—and more particularly his death—was actually of very great meaning. Abel the Nothing was most definitely a Something!

It is important to consider why Abel was keeping sheep. One thing he was unlikely to be keeping sheep for was to produce lamb chops. God had created all people and higher animals to eat only plants. We read about this in Genesis 1:29,30.

> And God said, "See, I have given you eve-ry herb that yields seed which is on the face of all the earth, and every tree whose fruit yields seed; to you it shall be for food. Also, to every beast of the

earth, to every bird of the air, and to everything that creeps on the earth, in
which there is life, I have given every
green herb for food"; and it was so.

It might seem odd to think that all animals
should eat plants. Interestingly, most meat-
eaters are really omnivores—animals that eat
both plants and other animals. Bears
probably eat a lot more plant material than
meat. But what about cats? Aren't they
nearly completely carnivorous?

As far as people are concerned, the
requirement to eat only plants was not lifted
until after the Flood, although it is likely that
many animals had started to eat meat. It is
possible that people too had begun to eat
meat before the Flood, because we know that
they were not obeying God. However, it is
unlikely that Abel would be among their
number, because the Bible describes him as a
man of faith in Hebrews 11:4 and as
"righteous Abel" in Matthew 23:35.

So, if Abel was not keeping these sheep for
food, then what was he keeping them for?

The answer is to do with Adam's
wardrobe! What did the well-dressed man or
woman of the first few years wear? Was it a
line in fig leaves? No! Adam and Eve dressed

themselves in fig leaves after their sin, believing this would hide their guilt. But God sees all and knows all and nothing can be hidden from him. It was at this point that God gave the three curses—on the serpent, on the woman and on the man. But we know that we can never cover our own guilt. So after God had declared the three curses of Genesis chapter 3, we read:

> Also for Adam and his wife the LORD God made tunics of skin, and clothed them. (Genesis 3:21)

In order that Adam and Eve's guilt be covered, it became necessary to use animal skins, resulting in the shedding of blood. Ultimately, the shedding of blood meant atonement for sin. That shows how serious sin is. We cannot cover our own guilt. We need God to do it for us, and that covering requires the shedding of blood—in its New Testament fulfilment, it requires the shedding of the blood of Jesus once for all on the cross. The blood of animals could never *forgive* sins; it could only cover them. It is only the blood of the Lamb of God—Jesus Christ—that can actually provide forgiveness of sin.

It is most likely, therefore, that Abel was keeping sheep, in order to supply skins for clothes. The point about the need for blood, as a covering for sin, was clearly not lost on Abel. That is what was so special about his offering to the LORD. He offered to the LORD "the firstborn of his flock and of their fat." Abel got it! He was open to and understood the fact that he was a sinner, who needed forgiveness—which at that time could only be achieved through the concept of animal sacrifice.

We can infer that Abel must have understood the need for the atoning blood of his sacrifices, as a covering for sin. In other words, Abel was a priest. A priest was someone who offered the blood sacrifices for the sins of the people. It is likely that Abel kept sheep in order to provide the clothing and in order to provide sacrifices.

Although this whole idea of blood sacrifices seems complicated to us—and also rather gruesome!—we can understand that the whole purpose was to point us towards the perfect fulfilment of the blood sacrifices: Jesus Christ. The unpleasantness of the blood sacrifices reminds us how unpleasant our sin is to God. The fact of Jesus' sacrifice once-for-all on the cross reminds us of how serious our sin is to God, and how much He loves us, in being prepared to take the punishment for our sins.

"The LORD did not respect Cain and his offering"

When I first heard the story of Cain and Abel, I was confused as to why one offering should be accepted and the other not. I had picked up entirely the wrong message from the story. No one had explained the significance of Abel's offering as a blood sacrifice. So no one explained why Cain's offering was wrong. Therefore, I grew up ignorant of the truth about why God had chosen to accept Abel, but to reject Cain. It just seemed to me that God was playing favourites with the two brothers, and that the story's moral was that you'd better just accept what God wants, whether you understand it or not! This interpretation gave me a false picture of God, How were we supposed to know what was acceptable? I was left wondering if what I was doing was acceptable and if not, what would become of me.

I wonder if my Sunday School teachers or my parents knew that this was the message I was picking up. Would they have been horrified? Or did they themselves not understand why God was perfectly fair and just in refusing to accept Cain's offering?

Maybe their teaching had not equipped them with the knowledge to impart the important message of this chapter of Genesis.

We have already learned that Abel was offering a sacrifice on behalf of sins. Just as Adam and Eve's new clothes were a covering for sin, as the result of the shedding of blood, so also Abel's sins were covered by his blood sacrifice. The purpose of blood sacrifice is to point us to Jesus—the ultimate and final blood sacrifice. This is why we learn in the book of Hebrews that:

And according to the law almost all things are purified with blood, and without shedding of blood there is no remission. (Hebrews 9:22)

The word remission refers to the removal of sins, by the atoning sacrifice of blood. Thus, without blood, there is no forgiveness.

Cain's offering did not involve blood. Therefore, by definition, it could not grant him forgiveness. Cain's offering was "of the fruit of the ground". It was an offering to the LORD, but it could not get him right with God. Cain was probably offering the very best that he could offer. But the best that we can do is not good enough for God. God has a pass mark, when He examines us. That pass mark is 100%. We just cannot achieve that pass mark by ourselves, and the sooner we realise this, the better. Indeed, the Bible tells us that "all our righteousnesses are like filthy rags" (Isaiah 64:6) There isn't actually anything that we can do to get ourselves right with God. We are sinners in His sight, deserving His wrath and condemnation. Remission of sins is gained only by the covering blood sacrifice— and today we mean the blood of Jesus Christ.

This is a hard truth to accept. We instinctively feel that there must be something we can do to get ourselves right with God. There isn't. If there were, then God would not have all the glory for our salvation. If we expect that something we do ourselves actually contributes towards our salvation, then this takes away a little from what God has done for us.

I have heard some Sunday School teachers tell their charges that God could see into Cain's heart, even though the Bible doesn't tell us what Cain was thinking. This is only half-true. It is correct that God can see into the heart, and that He knew Cain's heart was not right with Him. But we can actually work out from the text that Cain was not right with God. If Cain had been right with God, he would have offered a blood sacrifice, or maybe given his best crops to Abel in exchange for Abel's offering another sacrifice on Cain's behalf. But either of these options would have required humility on Cain's part, and his later actions show that humility was not one of his qualities. Instead, he tried to do everything his own way, by his own strength. If we also try to get ourselves right with God by our own efforts, however commendable they may seem on the surface, we will always fail. We cannot come to God in our own righteousness, but only in the righteousness of the "Lamb who was slain" on our behalf—the Lord Jesus Christ.

"The LORD said to Cain, 'Why are you angry?'"

Why did God ask Cain a question? Why does God ever ask questions? Surely He, who is infinite, all-powerful, all-knowing and all-present, cannot be asking for the sake of information! God knew, and God knows, the answer to every question before it is asked.

So I ask again, why does God use questions?

To understand why God uses questions, it might be useful to look back at the first questions that He asked.

The very first question that God asked is recorded in Genesis 3:9. He asked Adam "Where are you?" This seemingly innocent question is of profound importance.

Previous to this question, God and Adam had easy communion in the Garden of Eden. This is strongly implied, by the action of God's bringing the animals to Adam, in order for Adam to name them. Also, look at Genesis 3:8.

> And they heard the sound of the LORD God walking in the garden in the cool of the day.

It is interesting that God is described as "walking". This suggests that He was in human form at this point. There are many other places in the Old Testament where we see a human appearance of God, before Jesus came to the Earth. Jesus always was God, even prior to the creation of the world. In John's Gospel, we read:

> In the beginning was the Word, and the Word was with God, and the Word was God. He was in the beginning with God. All things were made through Him, and without Him nothing was made that was made. In Him was life, and the life was the light of men. And the light shines in the darkness, and the darkness did not comprehend it. (John 1:1-5)

It is, of course, Jesus who is being referred to as "the Word". It is through Him that the world was made. It is with Jesus that we have fellowship.

However, Genesis 3:8 shows that the fellowship was broken. The verse implies that it was God's usual practice to walk in the Garden. Surely, Adam and Eve should have welcomed this. Instead, we read:

Adam and his wife hid themselves from
the presence of the LORD God among
the trees of the garden. (Genesis 3:8)

So, when God asked them "Where are
you?" it was not because He didn't know. It
was because He wanted to give them the
opportunity to admit their guilt and to repent.

Returning to Genesis 4, God was doing the
same thing with Cain. He gave Cain the
opportunity to repent.

"Why are you so angry? And why has your
countenance fallen?" said God, in Genesis 4:6.
God knew what was in Cain's heart. He
entreats Cain that "If you do well, will you not
be acceptable?" Cain's offerings could be
accepted by God, if they were brought in the
right spirit, and involved the covering of
blood, which brings remission.

In the same way, it is always God's desire
that we should repent, rather than be
punished. He is angry with our sin, yet He
gives us every opportunity to repent and turn
to Him.

A History of Death

This story is most shocking, when you read it, believing all of Genesis to be true. Murder is always shocking. But the world's first ever murder must have been extra especially shocking.

But the death of Abel was not even just the world's first murder—it was the world's first death of a human being. That makes the event world-shatteringly shocking!

If Genesis is not literally true, then the account of Cain and Abel loses all its poignancy and significance. It was Tennyson who, in his poem "In Memoriam", described nature as "red in tooth and claw". The implication is that death is a *natural* part of *nature*. He implies that in a strange way, death is the means by which we get life. The theory of evolution requires the continual death of animals, so that later generations can exhibit acquired features and behaviours. Evolutionary history requires death from the beginning and further death in the future.

The Bible's history of death is different. The Bible looks forward to a time when there will be no death. Paul says "The last enemy that will be destroyed is death" (1 Corinthians 15:26). How will this death be conquered?

"For He (Jesus) must reign till He has put all enemies under His feet." (1 Corinthians 15:25). The last book of the Bible, Revelation, tells us that eventually death will be "cast into the lake of fire" (Revelation 20:14).

So the Bible expects us to look forward to a future without death. That is because we can look back to a past that had no death. Death was promised as a consequence, should Adam ever break the one commandment he had been given.

> And the LORD God commanded the man, saying, "Of every tree of the garden you may freely eat; but of the tree of the knowledge of good and evil you shall not eat, for in the day that you eat of it you shall surely die. (Genesis 2:16, 17)

People were not originally intended to die, in God's perfect world—but in the perfect world God had made, animals were not intended to die either.

> And God said, "See, I have given you every herb that yields seed which is on the face of all the earth, and every tree whose fruit yields seed; to you it shall be

for food. Also, to every beast of the earth, to every bird of the air, and to eve-rything that creeps on the earth, in which there is life, I have given every green herb for food"; and it was so. Then God saw everything that He had made, and indeed it was very good. So the evening and the morning were the sixth day. (Genesis 1:29-31)

We read this passage earlier, and showed that it meant that people and higher animals were designed to eat plants, not meat. This emphasises the point that there was to be no death in the world. Death is indeed an enemy.

With that history of death in mind, try re-reading what happened between Cain and Abel, and you will realise the seriousness of it.

Cain rose up against Abel his brother and killed him. (Genesis 4:8)

This is not just an incidental event. This is not just one in a long line of deaths. This is the absolute confirmation of what Adam and Eve were told—there is now death in the world. The first human to die did not get the chance to live to old age. He was murdered by his brother. This is death. This is murder. This is violence on a scale unprecedented and unforeseen by Adam. This is the proof that "the wages of sin is death" (Romans 6:23). The world's first death of a human would destroy our morale completely—if it weren't for the fact that the second half of Romans 6:23 reminds us that "but the gift of God is eternal life through Jesus Christ our Lord".

"I do not know. Am I my brother's keeper?"

Can there be any more insolent phrase in the Bible? One wonders at the audacity of Cain in his reply to God's question.

Perhaps before we study the conversation in detail, we ought to stop and marvel that the conversation took place at all. For someone as deep into sin as Cain, it is a wonder that God conversed with him at all. Cain was clearly no atheist. He knew that God existed—he spoke with Him. We shall see that Cain's idea of who God was had got considerably warped, but that God existed, there was no doubt.

We ought then to wonder at the fact that God asked Cain a question—"Where is Abel your brother?" We saw before that God asks questions in order to give the opportunity to repent. Could God really have been giving Cain another opportunity to repent? I believe the answer is "Yes". But Cain had just committed the world's first ever murder. Can murderers be saved? The answer would again seem to be "Yes".

This is very interesting. We saw earlier how it is not possible to please God by our own actions. We are sinners, and therefore need a

Saviour. All our sins keep us from God, so a very large sin, like murder, can just as easily be overcome by the blood of our Saviour as any other sin. This means that there will be murderers in heaven. We had better be ready for this shock, because it is the truth. There will be murderers in heaven, and there will be seemingly good people in hell—of course, they're not really good, because they are still short of God's pass mark.

If Cain was used to speaking with God, surely he must have known something about God. Surely he must have known that God knows everything. His previous conversation with God should have reminded him that God's questions were for Cain's benefit, not for God's. So, when God asked where Cain's brother was, why did Cain reply "I do not know"? Why did he try lying to God? He must have known that God knew.

If Cain really thought that God might not know what he had done, then there was clearly something faulty about Cain's knowledge about God. Is it too much to read into this that perhaps Cain thought that God was just a more advanced version of himself? Maybe he believed, as Mormons do today, that "as we are, God once was". He must certainly have decided that God was not omniscient (all-knowing).

Cain's second comment showed that not only did he not know God properly; that he didn't really know much *about* Him. He said "Am I my brother's keeper?" With this insolent comment, Cain was actually challenging God's right to question him. How dare God ask him where his brother is? After all, isn't this the same God, who had just shown favouritism, by accepting Abel's offering, but not his? Cain's actions and words show that he just didn't get it.

Do we think that we can pull the wool over God's eyes? Are we guilty of trying to hide our sins from Him? Do we not realise that this compounds our sins further?

It is true that there will be some murderers in heaven, but I suspect that Cain will not be one of them. This is because God gave him the opportunity to repent, but Cain did not do so. Instead, he demonstrated a lack of faith in God and a lack of knowledge about Him.

Henry Morris suggested that there was a sense in which Cain was correct, when he answered God's question—"where is Abel your brother"—by saying "I do not know". Abel had gone to be the first human occupant of Sheol, the place of the dead, referred to by

Jesus as "Abraham's bosom" (Luke 16:22). As a believer in God, saved by faith, Abel would, following Jesus' resurrection, be taken to be with Him in heaven. Cain might have known where Abel's body was, but he did not have, and would never have, any knowledge of God's saving grace, because of his failure to repent.

"What have you done? The voice of your brother's blood cries out to Me from the ground"

This time, God's question does not offer repentance. Repentance has been offered and rejected. We will look later at the result of deliberate rejection of the offer of repentance.

In this case, God's question is asked in order to show Cain the enormity of what he had done. There would be no point in this question, if there had already been human death, or if one person killing another had already happened. The question is asked, because this is the first ever murder and the first ever death of a human being.

But what does God mean about Abel's blood crying out from the ground? In order to understand this, we need to see what the New Testament says about Abel.

Jesus talked about Abel in Luke 11:49-51:

> Therefore the wisdom of God also said, 'I will send them prophets and apostles, and some of them they will kill and perse-cute,' that the blood of all the prophets which was shed from the foundation of

the world may be required of this generation, from the blood of Abel to the blood
of Zechariah who perished between the
altar and the temple. Yes, I say to you, it
shall be required of this generation.

Jesus described Abel as a prophet. Yet,
throughout the whole of the Bible, we have
no record of the prophecy of Abel. A prophet
is someone who speaks out God's words.
Where is the prophecy of Abel?

"The voice of your brother's blood cries
out to Me from the ground."

It is Abel's blood which is his prophecy. So
how can blood be a prophecy?
These are the things we need to know
about blood.
Humans and the higher animals all contain
blood. It is these that God chose to *bless* in
Genesis chapter 1. Forgive me—I will need to
be a little technical here. The Hebrew word
used in Genesis 1 as *bless* is the word
nephesh. Elsewhere in the Old Testament, the
word is translated as *life*. In fact, in Leviticus
17:11 we read "the life (*nephesh*)... is in the
blood. Therefore the blessing seems to be
linked with blood.

33

When Adam and Eve sinned, they tried to clothe themselves with fig leaves. This is like our trying to cover our own guilt. In fact, Adam and Eve's guilt could not be covered, until God had killed an animal to provide skins to clothe them. This first ever death of an animal occurred, in order to make a covering for sin. The first animal's death was as a direct consequence of sin.

The first ever death of a human being, therefore, was a prophecy. How could this be? Jesus described Abel as a prophet, but we have already seen that Abel was a priest. Not many people in the Bible hold the office of both prophet and priest. The most important figure to do so was, of course, Jesus. Therefore, just as the death of the first animal provided a covering for sin, the death of the first human pointed the way prophetically to the death of the Saviour, nearly 4000 years later.

Why did Cain suppose that his crime could be hidden from God? We do not know, although we have supposed that he had a faulty understanding of the nature of God. But the verse in the title of this section shows that nothing is hidden from God. Abel's blood was like a voice to God—it spoke of the shedding of blood to come, when the blood of God's own Son, Jesus, would be shed on the cross for our sins.

In the Old Testament, God sometimes appeared in human form. He did so to Abraham, for example, shortly before destroying Sodom and Gomorrah. The technical name for an Old Testament visitation of God in human form is a *theophany*. This rather unusual word is used, whenever we actually assume a pre-incarnate appearance of Jesus has taken place. In John's Gospel we read that Jesus is the Word, so it fair to assume that when God is conversing with people in the Old Testament, then this is actually a *theophany*—a pre-incarnate appearance of the Son of God. Therefore, it was Jesus Himself who was talking to Cain and telling him about his brother's blood crying out from the ground. That is why Jesus could so clearly speak about Abel's blood being a prophecy. It was to be God's Son who was to give His own blood as a punishment for our sins.

Abel was saved by faith

One of the most precious passages of the New Testament is Hebrews chapter 11. This passage is often called the "Hall of Faith". It lists great people of faith from the Old Testament. Hebrews 11 reminds us why we believe the early chapters of Genesis, along with the rest of the Bible.

> Now faith is the substance of things hoped for, the evidence of things not seen. For by it the elders obtained a good testimony. By faith we understand that the worlds were framed by the word of God, so that the things which are seen were not made of things which are visible. (Hebrews 11:1-3)

It is difficult for those of you who are not Christians to understand this issue of faith. One atheist has described faith as "believing something in the absence of evidence". Hebrews 11 is not talking about that. Faith does not require evidence. Faith actually **is** the evidence. It is by faith that we get to know God, and it is by faith that we know that God made the universe. That is why Hebrews 11 goes on to say:

But without faith it is impossible to please Him, for he who comes to God must believe that He is, and that He is a rewarder of those who diligently seek Him. (Hebrews 11:6)

The Bible tells us that we walk by faith, not by sight. We can never be saved by our own actions. The apostle Paul put it succinctly:

For by grace you have been saved through faith, and that not of yourselves; it is the gift of God, not of works, lest anyone should boast. (Ephesians 2:8,9)

We saw before that Abel's offering was acceptable to God, because he offered a blood sacrifice. Hebrews 11 lets us in on the secret as to why he offered this blood sacrifice, as a covering for sin.

By faith Abel offered to God a more excellent sacrifice than Cain, through which he obtained witness that he was righteous, God testifying of his gifts; and through it he being dead still speaks. (Hebrews 11:4)

Abel's offering was "more excellent" because of his faith. Abel's offering was not more acceptable, because he was a better quality human being. Abel's righteousness came through faith alone. This was the wonderful truth that Martin Luther understood, when he studied Romans, and reached where it says "The just shall live by faith" (Romans 1:17, quoting Habakkuk 2:4). This was the truth that sparked the Reformation. It was Abel's faith that gave him "witness" that he was right with God. If we were just to try and get right with God by our own methods, we could never make it. God's pass mark is 100%. We would never have any hope. Even if we could balance the good things we had done against our failings, how could we be sure that we had made it? We would have no comfort or assurance. The truth is that it is by grace that we are saved, through faith. It is part and parcel of believing that we are sinners, and therefore deserving of God's wrath. Abel knew that blood was needed to atone for (cover) his sin. We do not need to make a blood sacrifice. It has been done for us. We have already read that the death of Abel points us to Jesus, and it is Jesus' blood which was shed "once for all" upon the cross that makes it so that we do not need to offer another sacrifice.

I don't know how your church runs, but in my church, the pastor does not start the service by sacrificing a young lamb. Have you noticed that? There is no need to do so, because Jesus is the perfect Lamb of God— the Lamb who was slain, taking our punishment on the cross. What He requires from us is to repent—to turn thoroughly from our sins, and to turn to Him, who has taken the penalty that we deserve.

"Now you are cursed from the earth"

What a dreadful word the word *curse* is! In the Bible, if a man curses another, it expresses a desire for the recipient's hurt. However, when God curses someone, it is not merely a desire—the punishment described in the curse actually happens. The consequences on the individual are serious. For example, in Deuteronomy 29:20, God pronounces a curse on those that fail to keep His covenant.

> The LORD would not spare him; for then the anger of the LORD and His jealousy would burn against that man, and every curse that is written in this book would settle on him, and the LORD would blot out his name from under heaven.

Unlike people, God can curse objects, and they too will bear the consequences. For example, In Mark 11, Jesus comes across a fig tree, which is not in fruit when it should be. So He cursed it, with these words: "Let no one eat fruit from you ever again." (Mark

11:14). When the disciples see the tree later, they notice that it has withered.

> Peter, remembering, said to Him, "Rabbi, look! The fig tree which You cursed has withered away." (Mark 11:21)

Jesus has the authority to curse like this, because He is God, and therefore the author of creation.

This curse on the fig tree is therefore similar to the curse placed on Adam, in Genesis 3:17-19:

> Cursed is the ground for your sake; In toil you shall eat of it All the days of your life. Both thorns and thistles it shall bring forth for you, And you shall eat the herb of the field. In the sweat of your face you shall eat bread Till you return to the ground, For out of it you were taken; For dust you are, And to dust you shall return.

The curse placed on Adam has affected the whole of creation. As we read in Romans 8:20, 21:

> For the creation was subjected to futility,
> not willingly, but because of Him who
> subjected it in hope; because the crea-
> tion itself also will be delivered from the
> bondage of corruption into the glorious
> liberty of the children of God.

The curse to be placed on Cain was going to be extensive in scope, throughout his lifetime. It would involve his ability to farm, to grow crops and to settle down. After Adam's sin, God had cursed the earth. Now Cain was cursed *from* the earth.

This book is about the eternal consequences of whether or not we have faith. Surely, the important issue is therefore what would happen to Cain after he died, not what would happen to him for the rest of his life. Although that is true to a certain extent, what this account is teaching us is that there are consequences for sin here and now. For example, there are eternal consequences to a sin like adultery, but there are also consequences that the adulterer has to suffer here and now—broken relationships, destruction of trust, damage to children etc. God is making clear here in Genesis 4 that Cain's sin of murder, and also his lack of repentance, is something that will blight his life on earth, as well as his future eternity. Perhaps today such a link between earthly lives and God's curse is not so apparent, but it was vitally important for God to emphasise this link at such an early stage of the earth's history.

"My punishment is greater than I can bear!"

God had given Cain many opportunities to see his sin for what it was—and to repent. We have already found out that God's questions to Cain demonstrated His mercy. When He asks questions, it is not because He does not know the answer—it is because He is facilitating a response from us.

Now at last Cain made a response of some sort. In verse 13 we read:

> And Cain said to the LORD, "My punish-
> ment is greater than I can bear!"

It would appear that at long last Cain shows some measure of sorrow for his sin. Yet even now, his sorrow is not repentance. How can that be? Surely, we are told that repentance is saying sorry for our sins?

In fact, repentance is far more than merely saying sorry. We know from observing our children (and also many adults!) that it is possible to say sorry without really meaning it, or to be sorry that we have been found out, rather than sorry for what we have done.

Read Cain's declaration of sorrow carefully. You will see that this is not really repentance from sin.

> Surely You have driven me out this day from the face of the ground; I shall be hidden from Your face; I shall be a fugitive and a vagabond on the earth, and it will happen that anyone who finds me will kill me.

His concern is over what is going to happen to him. I must be wary, if it ever seems that my concern is merely about what will happen to me. This is sorrow with selfishness, which can never be a true form of repentance.

There are four elements to Cain's complaint about his punishment.

1. He will be driven away from the land that he tills.
2. He will be hidden from God's face.
3. He will be a wanderer on the earth.
4. He is concerned that he himself might get killed.

Of these complaints, numbers one, three and four are entirely selfish. Number four, in particular, is a justifiable concern. Since Cain himself has seen fit to commit the world's first murder, it is possible that someone else might have thought he was an easy target to kill. Cain's murder could easily be seen as a precedent and it is for this reason that God placed a mark on Cain so that people would not be able to kill him.

Cain's second complaint—that he will be hidden from God's face—seems to be a legitimate complaint. But what did he expect? Did he think that he could continue to have fellowship with God, when he can't even tell God the truth, even though he knows that God knows everything? God had already warned Cain that "If you do well, will you not be accepted? And if you do not do well, sin lies at the door. And its desire is for you, but you should rule over it." (Genesis 4:7) The warning should have been sufficient, but, as we have seen, God even gave Cain the opportunity to repent after he had committed murder—an opportunity Cain did not take.

There is always a danger of mistaking being sorry for being repentant. They are not the same. Feeling regret for the consequences that our sin has brought us is not repentance, even if we understand that it is God who brings about those consequences. Repentance is being genuinely sorry to God that we have sinned against Him, and turning away from that sin. It is this repentance that brings us salvation. This has always been the means of getting right with God, since the time of the very first sin—as the apostle Peter reminds us:

> Repent therefore and be converted, that your sins may be blotted out, so that times of refreshing may come from the presence of the Lord, and that He may send Jesus Christ, who was preached to you before, whom heaven must receive until the times of restoration of all things, which God has spoken by the mouth of all His holy prophets since the world began. (Acts 3:19-21)

"And the LORD set a mark on Cain, lest anyone finding him should kill him"

There has been a lot of speculation—indeed, too much speculation—about the way that Cain was marked. There have been white, racist 'Christians' who have claimed that Cain was marked by turning his skin black. (I put the word 'Christian' in inverted commas, because I do not accept any form of racism to be biblically valid, and therefore there is something suspect about the 'Christianity' of those who hold to such views).

This view would not seem to make sense. The purpose of the mark was so that people would not kill Cain. Yet, if the racists were right, and most humanity at the time was white, but Cain was black, why would that be any reason for people not to kill him? Indeed, surely it would make him more vulnerable to being found and killed.

In fact, the apostle Paul makes clear, in Acts 17, that we are all descended from "one blood". The differences in skin colour today are nothing to do with Cain and his mark. If you want to know more about the reasons for different people groups, skin colours and facial characteristics, read the *New Answers Book*.

Another view, sometimes held by the same people as that above, is that Cain was not actually Adam's son. Their claim is that Eve's sin was not really eating a fruit. These people claim that the fruit was a euphemism for sexual intercourse. Therefore, Eve's sin was actually adulterous intercourse with the devil. The claim is then made that Cain was the result of this coupling. The same people will then often go on to claim that blackness of skin is the mark of Cain, and that his descendents survived the Flood, meaning that they have to believe the Flood was limited to one area, rather than spreading out over the world.

This view also flies in the face of reality. It is much more sensible to assume that Eve's sin was actually in eating the fruit, because this action was deliberately forbidden by God. Indeed, the context of Genesis 4:1 suggests strongly that Adam must have been Cain's father.

Now Adam knew Eve his wife, and she conceived and bore Cain...

The conception of Cain follows directly from the intercourse between Adam and Eve, as we would expect.

There are so many fanciful ideas about the mark of Cain that we tend to overlook the obvious. We are not told what the mark was. We are not told, indeed, that it was anything physical. Indeed, the Hebrew word *oth*, from which it is translated, is better rendered as *sign* rather than *mark*. It is perfectly possible, therefore, that his mark was some sort of a badge or medal—though I acknowledge that this is just speculation. Whatever the sign was, it was something to bring reassurance to Cain. It could not have been anything that would bring more problems to Cain. Whatever the mark was, it was a protection. The mark of Cain illustrates God's incredible love, even towards sinners that will not repent.

"Then Cain went out from the presence of the Lord..."

There are many verses in the Bible, from which we draw great comfort. Many of these are to be found in Genesis. For example, later in Genesis, we find out that Noah was saved from the Flood simply because he found grace in the eyes of the Lord, and because he was a man of faith—not because he achieved some great level of goodness, which is unattainable for us today.

There are other verses in the Bible, which cause us alarm and concern. I suggest that the verse that I have used as the heading for this chapter is one of those alarming verses.

When I was at school, many years ago, we sometimes had to analyse sentences, by breaking them down into grammatical sections. With some sentences, this could help us understand more clearly what was meant. Let's try that exercise on the heading.

"Then..."

These actions happened subsequent to Cain's conversation with God. The word "then" also implies that there is a causal link. Cain going out from God's presence was caused by, and was the direct result of, both God's judgment on Cain, and Cain's failure to repent.

"Cain went out..."

51

This action was Cain's action. It was not God's action. We do not read that God withdrew Himself from Cain. Instead, it was Cain who went out. It was Cain who initiated the separation from God. He had initiated this separation earlier, by his sin, and by his failure to repent of his sin, even when given every opportunity to do so.

"...from the presence of the LORD..."

Cain was absenting himself from the presence of the LORD. This always reminds me of the account in the Gospels, where Jesus heals the man called Legion; his name meant that he was possessed by a large number of demons. You can read about the story in Luke 8:26-39. This man lived in the region known as the Gaderenes. Jesus delivered the man of his demons. As they left him, the demons begged to be allowed to go into the herd of pigs that the local people were keeping. As soon as Jesus had permitted them to do so, the pigs all ran down a steep hill into Lake Galilee and drowned.

The people from the town came to see what had happened. They saw the formerly demon-possessed man now in his right mind, sitting at Jesus' feet, listening to his teachings. At such evidence of Jesus' power, you might have thought that the locals would invite

Jesus into the town, to teach and preach. Not a bit of it! Instead they asked Jesus to depart from them. They wanted nothing to do with miracles from God. They were afraid, because seeing such miracles underlined their own lack of holiness, and their own sin. But the most frightening thing in the story for me is that Jesus does not stop to argue with them. When He was asked to leave, He left! These people, though they did not know it and would not have acknowledged it, had been in the presence of the LORD. They had witnessed God's power at first hand, and had asked Him to leave!

Cain, also, had been in the presence of the LORD. He had known what it was to talk with God. He had witnessed true worship from his brother. Although he had committed such a vile sin, nevertheless God, in His mercy, had given Cain the opportunity of salvation. Cain did not take it, but, instead, chose the path of rejecting God. The alarming thing about the verse is this: there may come a time beyond which you cannot be saved. There may come a time when your heart is too hardened to respond to God. Don't leave your repentance until then. Don't leave it until it is too late.

"Cain... dwelt in the land of Nod on the east of Eden"

Have you read the last few things that happened to Cain?

> Then Cain went out from the presence of the LORD and dwelt in the land of Nod on the east of Eden. And Cain knew his wife, and she conceived and bore Enoch. And he built a city, and called the name of the city after the name of his son—Enoch. (Genesis 4:16-17)

There are a lot of people who seem to like to spend time deliberately trying to find fault with the Bible. Such people will often stop at these verses. A number of different ideas have grown up around these verses.

The first issue that some people have a problem with is this. Who was Cain's wife? I have often been asked that question. In fact, I am usually asked it in this way. "So, then, Mr. Clever Creationist! Who was Cain's wife then? Aha! I bet you've never thought of that one before!"

I'm obviously exaggerating a bit, but there are many people who assume that this is the killer question.

There are a number of answers that they expect. One group of people assume that Adam and Eve only had two sons, called Cain and Abel. Therefore Cain's wife must have been from another family. Therefore there were more families. Therefore they probably all evolved anyway.

This view is easily refuted. The Bible actually names three sons of Adam and Eve. The third son was Seth. However, there must also have been children, whose names the Bible does not give. In Genesis 5:4, we read "The days of Adam after he fathered Seth were 800 years; and he had **other sons and daughters**." (ESV, emphasis mine). Therefore, it is perfectly rational and consistent to argue that all people were descended from these sons and daughters of Adam and Eve. Thus, it can be presumed that Cain's wife was one of his sisters.

But, but but...! Doesn't that mean that you creationists are condoning incest?

Of course it doesn't! Marriage between very close relations was condemned under the Mosaic Law—i.e. such relationships were not outlawed until the time of Moses. Indeed, Abraham's wife, Sarah, was his half-sister. We need to understand why such laws were ordained by God. Such close inter-marriage today can cause an increased likelihood of both parents sharing similar harmful genetic mutations, and therefore passing these on to their children. But Cain and his wife were only the second generation. Therefore, the genetic mutations had not yet risen to sufficiently dangerous levels. It would therefore be genetically safer for Cain to marry his sister than for two supposedly unrelated people in the same village today to get married.

Part of the problem that people have with these passages is that no indication is given about the timescales involved. The usual thinking is that when Cain killed Abel they were the only two children around. This is unlikely. They were probably grown up by this stage, in which case some of the other sons and daughters may well already have been born, and Abel might have been performing blood sacrifices on their behalf. The only chronological statement we can make is that the birth of Seth must have occurred after the murder of Abel, because Eve said "God has appointed another seed for me instead of Abel, whom Cain killed." Therefore, there is no reason to suppose that the population was not already growing. Cain could easily have found a wife from among his sisters. Note also that there is no suggestion that Cain found his wife in Nod. It is a completely legitimate rendering of the passage to presume that Cain was already married at the time of his argument with Abel, and that he took his wife with him into exile.

Nod simply means "wandering". So Cain was set to wandering. He became, as God had told him, a fugitive and a vagabond. But he was marked so that no one would kill him.

Finding Abel's Faith

We have already seen that Abel was a prophet. His blood was the prophecy. As his was the first human blood ever shed, it points people towards the blood of Jesus. No other human had ever died before—and certainly no other human had ever had his blood spilt over the ground. The importance of his blood serves to remind us of the importance of the blood of Jesus. We have already seen that Abel was a priest. He was offering sacrifices on behalf of the sins of the people. Not many characters in the Bible are both prophet and priest at the same time. One individual who holds both these offices stands out—it is Jesus. Abel, the priest who offered blood sacrifices for the covering of sins, has his own blood shed. Although Abel's blood is not a sacrifice, it points the way towards the one whose blood is indeed an efficacious sacrifice.

We have also seen that Abel's sacrifice was not good in and of itself—it was good, because it showed the need for forgiveness by the shedding of blood, and was offered by a man who had faith in God.

It will be worth looking at one last passage of scripture that talks about Abel. It is found in Hebrews 12:22-24..

> But you have come to Mount Zion and to
> the city of the living God, the heavenly
> Jerusalem, to an innumerable company
> of angels, to the general assembly and
> church of the firstborn who are regis-
> tered in heaven, to God the Judge of all,
> to the spirits of just men made perfect,
> to Jesus the Mediator of the new cove-
> nant, and to the blood of sprinkling that
> speaks better things than that of Abel.

This passage reminds us of who we are coming to. The point is that God is so holy and so omnipotent that we cannot stand in His presence, in our own righteousness. We are sinners. We are law breakers. God gave us the Ten Commandments, to show us how much we need Him.

If you ask someone if he thinks he is a good person, he will often answer "Yes!" If you ask him if he has obeyed the Ten Commandments, he will often assume that he has. So try and test yourself against the Ten Commandments.

Have you ever told a lie? Most, if not all of us, would have to answer "Yes". This means that we have broken the 9th Commandment. We are liars. James said "For whoever shall keep the whole law, and yet stumble in one point, he is guilty of all." (James 2:10) We don't really need to examine any of the other commandments, because we have proved to be lost already. However, just to compound the misery:

Have you ever taken anything that doesn't belong to you? Then you are a thief. If you responded "No", then don't forget that we have already established that you are a liar!

You may not have committed the act of adultery, but Jesus said "I say to you that whoever looks at a woman to lust for her has already committed adultery with her in his heart." (Matthew 5:28)

Have you actually worshipped God fully, as the only God of your heart? Have you given Him the number one position in all that you do? If not, you have certainly broken the First Commandment.

From these few, we see that we are guilty and we have to stand before God on Judgment Day. And if He acts justly, He will condemn us to hell for all eternity. We need God's mercy and we need His grace.

It has been said that mercy is not being treated as we deserve, and grace is being treated how we don't deserve! If we stand before a judge, who has pronounced us guilty, our only hope is if someone else pays the penalty on our behalf. In other words, we need a Mediator.

Hebrews 12:24 reminds us that Jesus is that Mediator. He is the one who has paid the price of our sins, by a blood sacrifice of His own blood. That is why His blood speaks better things than that of Abel. Abel's blood spoke of the promise of a Saviour to come. Our Saviour's blood speaks of the forgiveness of sins.

Throughout this book, we have seen how we can have our sins forgiven. It is by repentance. We have seen that repentance doesn't just mean saying sorry. Cain was sorry, but he did not repent. In order to repent, you need to admit that you are a sinner, who has broken God's Law. You need to repent of those sins. And you need to come to Jesus and receive Him. As it says in John 1:12:

> But as many as received Him, to them He gave the right to become children of God, to those who believe in His name.

I cannot do this for you. Nor can I realistically give you a prayer to say. The next step is between you and God. I urge you to put down this book, examine your life by the

Ten Commandments, admit you are a sinner, repent and beg God for mercy, through Jesus Christ. Then you will—not *might* but *will*—be saved. That is why the blood of Jesus speaks to us of something better. Indeed, something amazing!

Cain and Abel, Worship and Sacrifice

11815403R00039

Printed in Great Britain
by Amazon.co.uk, Ltd.,
Marston Gate.